CW00328086

TEACHERS

A TRIBUTE

TEACHERS

A TRIBUTE

Edited by Bridget Sullivan

Ariel Books

Andrews and McMeel

Kansas City

Illustrations © 1996 by Maura Fadden Rosenthal

ISBN: 0-8362-1056-5

Library of Congress Catalog Card Number: 95-80743

Introduction

Everyone who remembers his own educational experience remembers teachers, not methods and techniques.

—*Sidney Hook*

This lovely book is a heartfelt tribute to teachers, those hardworking individuals who help shape your education and your life. Who can forget the math teacher who was there for extra help when you needed it, the English teacher who introduced you to your favorite author, or the biology professor who stood by your side as you struggled to accomplish what at first seemed impossible?

Education does not cease the day we leave the classroom, nor are teachers only those who lecture to us in front of blackboards. Teachers come in all conceivable forms: the newspaper columnist who examines an issue in a way you have never seen before, the basketball coach who makes you truly understand the value of discipline and teamwork, the child who trots home from school and tells *you* something you never knew about astronomy, Guatemala, or snowflakes.

You are a teacher yourself when you show your son how to throw a ball, when you help your daughter sew her first pattern, or when you demonstrate to a colleague how to use a new wrench or an updated computer program. To all of us teachers, then—those of us who instruct as a livelihood, as well as those of us who teach in other ways—this book offers guidance, insight, and understanding into one of the world's oldest and most noble professions.

Morrow

ield T

ring b

Teachers

As with all great teachers, his curriculum was an insignificant part of what he communicated. From him you didn't learn a subject, but life. . . . Tolerance and justice, fearlessness and pride, reverence and pity, are learned in a course on long division if the teacher has those qualities, . . .

—*William Alexander Percy*

My heart is singing for joy this morning. A miracle has happened! The light of understanding has shone upon my little pupil's mind, and behold, all things are changed!

—*Annie Sullivan*

Teachers
believe they
have a gift for
giving; it drives
them with the same
irrepressible drive that
drives others to create a
work of art or a market or a
building. —*A. Bartlett Giamatti*

What constitutes the teacher is the
passion to make scholars.
—*George Herbert Palmer*

Don't try to fix the students, fix our-
selves first. The good teacher makes
the poor student good and the good
student superior. When our students
fail, we, as teachers, too, have failed.
—*Marva Collins*

I was still learning when I taught my
last class.

—*Claude M. Fuess,*
after forty years of teaching

A teacher affects eternity; he can never
tell where his influence stops.
—*Henry Adams*

To teach is to learn.

—Japanese proverb

The most extraordinary thing about a really good teacher is that he or she transcends accepted educational methods.

—*Margaret Mead*

My joy in learning is partly that it enables me to teach.

—*Seneca*

Everywhere I go I'm asked if I think the university stifles writers. My opinion is that they don't stifle enough of them. There's many a bestseller that could have been prevented by a good teacher.

—*Flannery O'Connor*

To be sure, there is an age-old prejudice against teaching. . . . Even a politician stands higher, because power in the street seems less of a mockery than power in the classroom. But when we speak of Socrates, Jesus, Buddha, and "other great teachers of humanity," the atmosphere somehow changes and the politician's power begins to look shrunken and mean. August examples show that no limit can be set to the power of a teacher, but this is equally true in the other direction: no career can so nearly approach zero in its effects.

—*Jacques Barzun*

When a teacher calls a boy by his
entire name it means trouble.

—Mark Twain

The only good teachers for you are
those friends who love you, who think
you are interesting, or very important,
or wonderfully funny.

—Brenda Ueland

A teacher must believe
in the value and interest
of his subject as a doctor
believes in health.

—Gilbert Highet

The true teacher defends his pupils against his own personal influence.

—*A. Bronson Alcott*

Human beings are full of emotion, and the teacher who knows how to use it will have dedicated learners. It means sending dominant signals instead of submissive ones with your eyes, body, and voice.

—*Leon Lessinger*

Teacher: The child's third parent.

—*Hyman Maxwell Berston*

Teachers are expected to reach unattainable goals with inadequate tools. The miracle is that at times they accomplish this impossible task.

—*Haim G. Ginot*

It is the supreme art of the teacher to awaken joy in creative expression and knowledge.

—*Albert Einstein*

The mediocre teacher tells. The good teacher explains. The superior teacher demonstrates. The great teacher inspires.

—*William Arthur Ward*

The teacher's life should have three periods—study until twenty-five, investigation until forty, profession until sixty, at which age I would have him retired on a double allowance.

—*Sir William Osler*

The teacher can consult outside of hours with his superiors or colleagues; he can get advice and talk over his difficulties. But when he goes into the classroom, shuts the door, takes the lonely seat behind the desk, and looks into the shining morning faces, then he is thrown back absolutely on himself. No power on earth can help him, and nothing can save the situation if he makes a blunder. There he needs all his resources, all his courage, and infinite patience.

—*William Lyon Phelps*

What was the duty of the teacher if not to inspire?

—*Bharati Mukherjee*

I see the mind of the five-year-old as a volcano with two vents: destructiveness and creativeness.

—*Sylvia Ashton-Warner*

Everyone who remembers his own educational experience remembers teachers, not methods and techniques. The teacher is the kingpin of the educational situation. He makes or breaks programs.

—*Sidney Hook*

If I had a child who wanted to be a teacher, I would bid him Godspeed as if he were going to a war. For indeed the war against prejudice, greed, and ignorance is eternal, and those who dedicate themselves to it give their lives no less because they may live to see some fraction of the battle won.

—*James Hilton*

Teacher: Two kinds: the kind that fill you with so much quail shot that you can't move, and the kind that just give you a little prod behind and you jump to the skies.

—*Robert Frost*

I have never heard anyone whom I consider a good teacher claim that he or she *is* a good teacher—in the way that one might claim to be a good writer or surgeon or athlete. Self-doubt seems very much a part of the job of teaching: one can never be sure how well it is going.

—*Joseph Epstein*

Teachers should unmask themselves, admit into consciousness the idea that one does not need to know everything there is to know and one does not have to pretend to know everything there is to know.

—*Esther P. Rothman*

A teacher is better than two books.

—*German proverb*

Good teachers are glad when a term begins and a little sad when it ends. They remember some of their students for many years, and their students remember them. They never make assumptions about what their pupils know; they take the trouble to find out, and they are tireless in finding new ways of repeating where repetition is necessary.

—*Margaret Mead*

The job of a teacher is to excite in the young a boundless sense of curiosity about life, so that the growing child shall come to apprehend it with an excitement tempered by awe and wonder.

—*John Garrett*

A good teacher, like a good entertainer first must hold his audience's attention. Then he can teach his lesson.

—*John Hendrik Clarke*

The first idea that the child must acquire in order to be actively disciplined is that of the difference between good and evil; and the task of the educator lies in seeing that the child does not confound good with immobility, and evil with activity.

—Maria Montessori

I touch the future. I teach.

—Christa McAuliffe

I'm not a teacher: only a fellow
traveler of whom you asked the way. I
pointed ahead—ahead of myself as
well as of you.

—*George Bernard Shaw*

Good teachers have a toehold on
immortality, which is only a word for
little islands in the rising tide of time.
    Islands remembered briefly, for
time's eventual tide gets us all. But
good teachers, I think, are longer
remembered over the brief tick tock of
decades; each man recalls his own.

—*John Keasler*

No bubble is so iridescent or floats
longer than that blown by the
successful teacher.

> —*Sir William Osler*

The truth is that I am enslaved . . . in one
vast love affair with seventy children.

> —*Sylvia Ashton-Warner*

If the heavens were all parchment, and
the trees of the forest all pens, and
every human being were a scribe, it
would still be impossible to record all
that I have learned from my teachers.

> —*Jochanan Ben Zakkai, attributed*

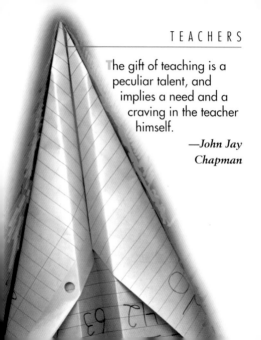

The gift of teaching is a
peculiar talent, and
implies a need and a
craving in the teacher
himself.

—*John Jay
Chapman*

When you are a teacher you are always in the right place at the right time. There is no wrong time for learning. It may be the wrong time for what the teacher had planned to teach, but just as certainly it will be the perfect time to teach something else. Teachers learn to grasp the moment. Any time a student is there before you, the possibility is present, the moment is yours.

—*Betty B. Anderson*

The teacher's task is not to implant facts but to place the subject to be learned in front of the learner and, through sympathy, emotion, imagination, and patience, to awaken in the learner the restless drive for answers and insights which enlarge the personal life and give it meaning.

—*Nathan M. Pusey*

Good teachers are costly, but bad teachers cost more.

—*Bob Talbert*

The schoolmaster is abroad, and I trust more to him, armed with his primer, against the soldier in full military array, for upholding and extending the liberties of his country.

—*Henry Brougham*

[A student] wants to feel that the instructor is not simply passing on dead knowledge in the form that it was passed on to him, but that he has assimilated it and has read his own experience into it, so that it has come to mean more to him than almost anything in the world.

—*Randolph Bourne*

Teachers who have plugged away at their jobs for twenty, thirty, and forty years are heroes. I suspect they know in their hearts they've done a good thing, too, and are more satisfied with themselves than most people are.

Most of us end up with no more than five or six people who remember us. Teachers have thousands of people who remember them for the rest of their lives.

—*Andrew A. Rooney*

I owe a lot to my teachers and mean to pay them back someday.

—Stephen Leacock

A good teacher is one who helps you become who you feel yourself to be. A good teacher is also one who says something you won't understand until ten years later.

—Julius Lester

He that teaches us anything which we knew not before is undoubtedly to be reverenced as a master.

—Samuel Johnson

One good teacher in a lifetime may sometimes change a delinquent into a solid citizen.

—*Philip Wylie*

One looks back with appreciation to the brilliant teachers, but with gratitude to those who touched our human feelings. The curriculum is so much necessary raw material, but warmth is the vital element for the growing plant and for the soul of the child.

—*Carl Jung*

Teachers are more than any other class
the guardians of civilization.

—*Bertrand Russell*

A successful teacher needs: the education of a college president, the execu-
tive ability of a financier, the humility
of a deacon, the adaptability of a
chameleon, the hope of an optimist,
the courage of a hero, the wisdom of
a serpent, the gentleness of a dove,
the patience of Job, the grace of God,
and the persistence of the Devil.

—*Anonymous*

I'm never going to be a movie star. But then, in all probability, Liz Taylor is never going to teach first and second grade.

—*Mary J. Wilson,*
elementary school teacher

Education

An education is not a thing one gets, but a lifelong process.

—*Gloria Steinem*

That is what learning is. You suddenly understand something you've understood all your life, but in a new way.

—*Doris Lessing*

The goal of education is the advancement of knowledge and the dissemination of truth.

—*John F. Kennedy*

here are few earthly things more beautiful than a university . . . a place where those who hate ignorance may strive to know, where those who perceive truth may strive to make others see.

—*John Masefield*

Minds are like parachutes: they only function when open.

—*Thomas R. Dewar*

Education then, beyond all other devices of human origin, is a great equalizer of the conditions of men,—the balance wheel of the social machinery.

—*Horace Mann*

Give a man a fish and you feed him for a day. Teach a man to fish and you feed him for a lifetime.

—*Chinese proverb*

If you promise not to believe everything
your child says happens at this school,
I'll promise not to believe everything he
says happens at home.

—*Anonymous*

In the education of children there is
nothing like alluring the interest and
affection; otherwise you only make so
many asses laden with books.

—*Michel de Montaigne*

The main part of intellectual education is not the acquisition of facts but learning how to make facts live.

—*Oliver Wendell Holmes Jr.*

I consider a human soul without education like marble in a quarry, which shows none of its inherent beauties until the skill of the polisher sketches out the colors, makes the surface shine, and discovers every ornamental cloud, spot, and vein that runs through it.

—*Joseph Addison*

The sweet and powerful knowledge we gain . . . should not close us back upon our narrow selves, but should make us truly "citizens of the world."

—*Nannerl O. Keohane*

It is a greater work to educate a child, in the true and larger sense of the word, than to rule a state.

—*William Ellery Channing*

In teaching it is the method and not the content that is the message . . . the drawing out, not the pumping in.

—*Ashley Montague*

Four years was enough of Harvard. I still had a lot to learn, but had been given the liberating notion that now I could teach myself.

—*John Updike*

If you educate a man you educate a person, but if you educate a woman you educate a family.

—*Ruby Manikan*

Teaching is an instinctual art, mindful of potential, craving of realizations, a pausing, seamless process.

—*A. Bartlett Giamatti*

It is important that students bring a certain ragamuffin, barefoot irreverence to their studies; they are not here to worship what is known, but to question it.

—*Jacob Bronowski*

And if education is always to be conceived along the same antiquated lines of a mere transmission of knowledge, there is little to be hoped from it in the bettering of man's future. For what is the use of transmitting knowledge if the individual's total development lags behind?

—*Maria Montessori*

That's what education means—to be able to do what you've never done before.

—*George Herbert Palmer*

As long as you live, keep learning how to live.

—*Seneca*

Good teaching is one-fourth preparation and three-fourths theater.

—*Gail Godwin*

But it is not hard work which is dreary; it is superficial work. That is always boring in the long run, and it has always seemed strange to me that in our endless discussions about education so little stress is ever laid on the pleasure of becoming an educated person, the enormous interest it adds to life. To be able to be caught up into the world of thought—that is to be educated.

—Edith Hamilton

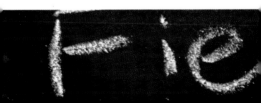

By learning you will teach; by teaching you will learn.

—Latin proverb

Education is leading human souls to what is best, and making what is best out of them; and these two objects are always attainable together. . . .

—John Ruskin

Respect for the fragility and importance of an individual life is still the first mark of the educated man.

—Norman Cousins

At the desk where I sit, I have learned one great truth. The answer for all our national problems—the answer for all the problems of the world—comes to a single word. That word is "education."

—*Lyndon B. Johnson*

We cannot always build the future for our youth, but we can build our youth for the future.

—*Franklin D. Roosevelt*

One may receive the information but miss the teaching.

—*Jean Toomer*

The important thing is not so much
that every child should be taught,
as that every child should be given the
wish to learn.

—*John Lubbock*

No one has yet fully realized the wealth of sympathy, kindness, and generosity hidden in the soul of a child. The effort of every true education should be to unlock that treasure.

—*Emma Goldman*

The secret of teaching is to appear to have known all your life what you learned this afternoon.

—*Anonymous*

It is one thing to show a man that he is in error, and another to put him in possession of truth.

—*John Locke*

In the long run of history, the censor and the inquisitor have always lost. The only sure weapon against bad ideas is better ideas. The source of better ideas is wisdom. The surest path to wisdom is a liberal education.

—*A. Whitney Griswold*

I maintain, in truth,
That with a smile we should instruct our
     youth,
Be very gentle when we have to blame,
And not put them in fear of virtue's
     name.

—*Molière*

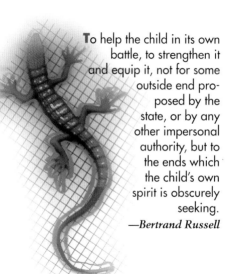

To help the child in its own battle, to strengthen it and equip it, not for some outside end proposed by the state, or by any other impersonal authority, but to the ends which the child's own spirit is obscurely seeking.

—*Bertrand Russell*

The object of teaching a child is to enable him to get along without a teacher.

—*Elbert Hubbard*

Fifty years ago teachers said their top discipline problems were talking, chewing gum, making noise, and running in the halls. The current list, by contrast, sounds like a cross between a rap sheet and the seven deadly sins. . . .

—*Anna Quindlen*

The art of teaching is the art of
assisting discovery.

—*Mark Van Doren*

Teaching was the hardest work I had
ever done, and it remains the hardest
work I have done to date.

—*Ann Richards*

On one occasion Aristotle was asked
how much educated men were superior
to those uneducated: "As much," said
he, "as the living are to the dead."

—*Diogenes Laertius*

Education is not a *product:* mark, diploma, job, money—in that order; it is a *process,* a never-ending one.
—*Bel Kaufman*

The object of education is to prepare the young to educate themselves throughout their lives.
—*Robert Maynard Hutchins*

To know how to suggest is the great art of teaching. To attain it we must be able to guess what will interest; we must learn to read the childish soul as we might a piece of music.

—*H. F. Amiel*

A good education should leave much to be desired.

—*Alan Gregg*

Teaching kids to count is fine, but teaching them what counts is best.

—*Bob Talbert*

The function of the university is not simply to teach bread-winning, or to furnish teachers for the public schools or to be a centre of polite society; it is, above all, to be the organ of that fine adjustment between real life and the growing knowledge of life, an adjustment which forms the secret of civilization.

—*W. E. B. DuBois*

The pupil who is never required to do what he cannot do, never does what he can do.

—*John Stuart Mill*

We might cease thinking of school as a place, and learn to believe that it is basically relationships between children and adults, and between children and other children. The four walls and the principal's office would cease to loom so hugely as the essential ingredients.

—*George Dennison*

It is not enough to have a good mind; the main thing is to use it well.

—*René Descartes*

Teach the young people how to think,
not what to think.

—*Sidney Sugarman*

Education is a private matter between
the person and the world of knowledge
and experience, and has little to do
with school or college.

—*Lillian Smith*

Anyone who stops learning is old, whether at twenty or eighty. Anyone who keeps learning stays young. The greatest thing in life is to keep your mind young.

—Henry Ford

To teach is to learn twice.

—Joseph Joubert

Children are unpredictable. You never know what inconsistency they're going to catch you in next.

—Franklin P. Jones

The classroom and teacher occupy the most important part, the most important position of the human fabric. . . . In the schoolhouse we have the heart of the whole society.

—*Henry Golden*

Education is helping the child realize his potentialities.

—*Erich Fromm*

Genius without Education is like Silver in the Mine.

—*Benjamin Franklin*

Education is a wonderful thing. If you couldn't sign your name you'd have to pay cash.

—*Rita Mae Brown*

Education is not the filling of a pail, but the lighting of a fire.

—*William Butler Yeats*

The potential possibilities of any child are the most intriguing and stimulating in all creation.

—*Ray L. Wilbur*

The schools of the country are its
future in miniature.

—*Tehyi Hsieh*

Our progress as a
nation can be no
swifter than our
progress in
education.

—*John F.
Kennedy*

Learning is discovering that something
is possible.

—*Fritz Perls*

A child must feel the flush of victory
and the heart-sinking of disappoint-
ment before he takes with a will to the
tasks distasteful to him and resolves to
dance his way through a dull routine of
textbooks.

—*Helen Keller*

A child miseducated is a child lost.

—*John F. Kennedy*

An educated man should know everything about something, and something about everything.

—*C. V. Wedgwood*

A liberal education is at the heart of a civil society, and at the heart of a liberal education is the act of teaching.

—*A. Bartlett Giamatti*

Teaching is the royal road to learning.

—*Jessamyn West*

What office is there which involves more responsibility, which requires more qualifications, and which ought, therefore, to be more honorable, than that of teaching?

—*Harriet Martineau*

Education begins at home. You can't blame school for not putting into your child what you don't put into him.

—*Geoffrey Holder*

It is hard to convince a high-school student that he will encounter a lot of problems more difficult than those of algebra and geometry.

—*Edgar W. Howe*

The things taught in schools are not an education but the means of an education.

—*Ralph Waldo Emerson*

The highest result of education is tolerance.

—*Helen Keller*

The whole art of teaching is only the
art of awakening the natural curiosity
of young minds for the purpose of
satisfying it afterwards.

—*Anatole France*

To teach is to touch
lives forever.

—*Anonymous*

The text of this book is set in
Futura and Berling Roman
by Mspace, Brooklyn, New York.

Book design by Maura Fadden Rosenthal

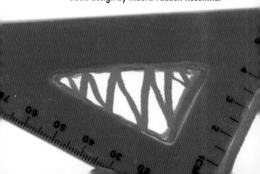